The 18th Hole
Stories from the U.S. Open at the Olympic Club, San Francisco, California
1955, 1966, 1987, 1998

———————————

Frank Doyle

The 18th Hole

Stories from the U.S. Open at the Olympic Club, San Francisco, California
1955, 1966, 1987, 1998

ISBN 978-0-9833882-1-0

For additional information, visit www.thewrongguyalwayswinsatolympic.com

Printed in the United States of America by

be here now books

Foreword

The Olympic Club, first named the San Francisco Olympic Club, is the oldest athletic club in the United States (established on May 6, 1860). On January 2, 1893 the club opened its first permanent clubhouse on Post Street. That building did not survive the San Francisco earthquake. The club includes three golf courses located at San Francisco's border with Daly City, California. The three courses at the Olympic Club are the Cliffs, Lake and Ocean courses. The Lake and Ocean are 18-hole par-71 courses, and the Cliff course is a nine-hole par-3 course that is on the bluffs of the Pacific Ocean. All three courses are lined with many trees *(almost 40,000 on the Lake course)* and offer views of the Golden Gate Bridge and Golden Gate Park.

The Olympic Club has hosted four U.S. Open Championships in 1955, 1966, 1987, and 1998. It is scheduled to host the U.S. Open again in 2012. Jack Fleck won the 1955 U.S. Open. He defeated Ben Hogan in an 18-hole playoff after the two had tied at the end of 72 holes with scores of 287. Billy Casper defeated Arnold Palmer in a playoff to capture the 1966

U.S. Open title. In 1987, Scott Simpson won the U.S. Open by one stroke over Tom Watson. Lee Janzen won the most recent U.S. Open at Olympic in 1998 with a score of 280 (even par, as the course played a par 70 for the U.S. Open).

The 18th Hole
Stories from the U.S. Open at the Olympic Club, San Francisco, California
1955, 1966, 1987, 1998

From the championship tees the 18th hole at the Olympic Club's Lake Course measures only 347 yards. It's a short par four by modern standards, and if you simply looked at the scorecard you would question whether it is a worthy finishing hole for a United States Open Golf Championship. Despite its rather diminutive yardage, in the four Opens the Lake Course has hosted, this beguiling bit of turf has been the scene of some of the most dramatic events in the championship's history.

In 1955, Jack Fleck rolled in a seven-foot putt on the 18th hole to force a playoff for the U.S. Open title with Ben Hogan, the greatest golfer in the world at that time. The Fleck vs. Hogan contest was but the first in a series of David and Goliath stories, which would both delight and haunt the U.S. Opens played at the Olympic Club.

In their head to head match the next day, the final hole would provide more drama. Hogan came to the tee-trailing Fleck by a single stroke. He proceeded to severely hook his drive to the left into deep rough on a hillside bordering the country club's tennis courts. Hogan's lie was impossible. There are images of Hogan addressing his shot with the weedy grass running up to his knees. It took Hogan three attempts to extricate his ball from that lie and he proceeded to make a six on the last hole of his playoff with Fleck and lost the match by three strokes.

Over the years there has been a lot of speculation over the reason for Hogan's errant shot. In 1955, Hogan was a notorious for the machine-like precision of his swing. He was also notorious for his relentless practice regimen. He was once quoted as saying; "There aren't enough hours in the day to practice all of the shots you need to practice in order to win golf championships."

To golf patrons, Hogan's breakdown on the 18th tee was inexplicable. A number of witnesses blamed the condition of the tee box for the mis-hit. The hole had been lengthened by twenty yards for the tournament and the new tee area contained a mixture of sand and dirt, which caused Hogan's left foot to slip on his downswing. Members of the golf intelligentsia reasoned that under the pressure of having to make up a stroke on the final hole, Hogan reverted to his old habit of "duck hooking" shots which had plagued him in the late 1930's and had almost caused him to quit playing professional golf. In any event, my father said that Hogan's drive on the 18th hole in the 1955 playoff posed a mythical question: "Did his foot slip, or did his heart flutter?"

In 1955, it was undisputed that Ben Hogan was the greatest golfer in the world. His legend was of mythical proportion. He was a veteran of World War II having served in the Army Air Corps until the war ended in 1945. He had survived a near fatal car crash in 1949. He had thrown himself across the driver's seat in order to shield his wife, Valerie, from the collision with a Greyhound Lines bus on a two-lane highway near El Paso, Texas. Doctors told him that it was unlikely that he would ever be able to play competitive golf again. Hogan, however, was determined to tee it up again and play at the highest competitive level. Colleagues and fans alike had always been amazed at his ability to exert his "will power" in order to achieve his goals. Despite the physical injuries, which would linger and plague him the rest of his life, Hogan rehabilitated both his body and his golf game. Miraculously, he won the United States Open the following year at Merion Country Club, outside of Philadelphia. He claimed Open titles again in 1951 and 1953. When he arrived at the Olympic Club in 1955, Hogan was seeking a record fifth United States Open title.

Destiny seems to have had Hogan's life converge with that of Jack Fleck. In his autobiography, Fleck eerily recounts the fact that his car passed the ambulance carrying Hogan away from the accident on that El Paso highway. Then there was the matter of the golf clubs. Seeking to secure a business future after his days as a professional golfer, Hogan started a golf club manufacturing business in his native Forth Worth. Fleck visited the factory, was granted an audience with Hogan himself; and purchased a set of Hogan's newly forged golf clubs. At the 1955 Open there were only two players in the field who played the clubs manufactured by Hogan: the man who manufactured them and Jack Fleck. On Tuesday, prior to the tournament, Hogan delivered to Fleck two new "equalizer" wedges and wished him the best of luck in the tournament.

The convergence of these two lives reached its apex on the 18th hole at the Olympic Club during the 1955 U.S. Open. Until 1965, competitors played two rounds on Saturday, which was the final day of the tournament unless there was a tie, which would result in an 18-hole playoff the next day. On that Saturday in 1955, Fleck had a troublesome morning round of 75. He, along with everyone else, believed that he had shot himself out of the tournament. However, in the afternoon round, Fleck caught fire. He approached the 15th tee needing to birdie two of his last four holes to tie Hogan, who on Saturday had shot steady rounds of 72 and 70. Fleck birdied the par-3 15th and then made par on the next two very difficult holes. He strode to the 18th tee needing a birdie to tie Hogan and force a playoff the next day.

In his autobiography, Fleck describes the scene: "As I walked to the 18th tee, I paused at the front tee and looked toward the 18th green, there was a natural amphitheater and a large crowd on both sides of the fairway, all the way up to the green, with the big clubhouse perched on the left side of the hill. The clouds moved quickly overhead and let a few streaks of sunlight shine through--what a sight! I said to myself, "If this isn't heaven, I don't know what is!"

Meanwhile, inside the clubhouse, Ben Hogan sat on a bench near his locker. He had packed up his things and arranged for the clubhouse porter to place his golf clubs into their travel bag. As he was contemplating his trip back to Fort Worth, a newspaper reporter approached him and informed him that Fleck had reached the 18th tee and needed a birdie to tie him for the championship. "I hope he either makes an eagle or a par," Hogan told the reporter as he took a drag from a freshly lit cigarette. The reporter left to watch Fleck play the final hole.

Jack Fleck hit a 3-wood off the tee. His ball veered left, but not severely, and landed in the first cut of rough just off the left side of the fairway. He chose to hit a 7-iron for his second shot, and he hit it perfectly within seven feet of the hole. One viewing a photograph of that shot in the newspaper, most people would swear that Ben Hogan himself was hitting it. Fleck's attire mirrored that of Hogan, as both men wore the same cotton newspaper boy caps. However, it is the position of Fleck's follow through which completes the impersonation. Psychologists have ruminated that on that Saturday and Sunday, Fleck's being transferred itself into Hogan's and he assumed Hogan's golf essence. In this altered state, Fleck calmly stroked his tricky, short side hill putt into the hole.

Hogan, on the other hand, didn't move a muscle. He just sat there finishing his smoke. When Hogan heard the boisterous roar of the crowd below, he ground his cigarette out in the ashtray next to him and told the porter to unpack his clubs and put them back into his locker, as he would need them the next day.

In 1955 Fleck was a true oddity among his fellow professional golfers. Until his victory over Hogan at Olympic, he had never won a golf tournament. In order to qualify to play in the 1955 U.S. Open, he had to survive local qualifying rounds, which he barely managed. He had essentially quit playing on the professional circuit and had devoted his efforts into managing the operations of two public golf courses in Davenport, Iowa. In addition to his lackluster record, Fleck's personal habits were viewed as eccentric. He had taken up the practice of Hatha yoga, and was very careful about his diet. These practices were in sharp contrast to the lifestyles of most golf professionals of his day, which often included heavy cigarette smoking, and the hefty consumption of hard liquor. Fleck credits his yoga discipline and his healthy eating habits to allowing him to remain calm and focused throughout his U.S. Open ordeal.

Ben Hogan never won another Open championship. He contended in 1960 at Cherry Hills where from tee to green his play lapped the field. However, his putting was atrocious, and his miscues on the green allowed Arnold Palmer to miraculously come from behind with some heroic play to snatch the U.S. Open title that year.

Eleven years later, in the final round of a second U.S. Open played at the Olympic Club's Lake Course, Arnold Palmer wobbled to the 18th tee like a prize fighter who had been pummeled by Rocky Marciano for fourteen rounds in a heavy weight fight. After building up a seven-stroke lead on the front nine of the course, Palmer had inexplicably squandered that lead and came to the 18th hole tied for the championship with his playing partner, Billy Casper.

Casper was no Jack Fleck. He lacked the electric charisma and charm of Palmer. In contrast to Palmer's athletic build, Casper was rather rotund, although over the year before the 1966 U.S. Open he had shed some thirty pounds of fat from his six-foot frame by excluding beef from his diet and substituting buffalo meat. As a consequence, certain sportswriters started referring to him in their columns as "Buffalo Bill."

His demeanor on the golf course was business like, if not stoic, a quality that some commentators attributed to his Mormon faith. Casper's play did not ignite either golf patrons or the media. Both groups found his game boring. Hole after hole, Casper would hit a medium length drive into the middle of the fairway and then follow with a crisp, straight iron shot to the middle of the green. His game lacked the heroic drama exhibited by Palmer's tremendous drives and great recovery shots from impossible lies. Palmer's self-proclaimed style of play was "go for broke", and Casper's was "steady as she goes." Perhaps no two golfers better portrayed the proverbial competition between the tortoise and the hare.

Almost to a man, touring professionals credited Palmer for the rise in golf's popularity in American sport. Arnold was good on television and television was good for golf. Among his contemporaries on the professional golf tour, however, Casper was regarded as the superior player. He had already won a U.S. Open in 1959 at the Wing Foot Golf Club in New York. Wing Foot sported a similar design and degree of difficulty to that posed by the Lake Course at the Olympic Club. His plodding style of play from tee to green did not provide the drama craved by television viewers, but it was impeccably effective. Once on the green, Casper was deadly and he was far and away the best putter on tour.

The way the two men played that final hole of the 1966 U.S. Open exemplified their contrasting styles. Casper was first to play since he made par on the difficult 17th hole and Palmer had taken a bogey. Casper hit a solid, but mundane drive into the middle of the fairway. Palmer addressed his ball and then swung for the fences with the desperation of a man trying to make the impossible happen. His ball rocketed left off of the tee into the deep rough on the hillside, far left of the fairway.

His position was eerily similar to where Hogan's tee shot had landed in 1955 in his playoff with Jack Fleck, and his lie was just as terrible. Palmer, however, took a wedge and with all his strength was able to hit one of his miraculous recovery shots 30 feet from the pin. Casper methodically hit a crisp; eight-iron shot some fifteen feet below the hole. Palmer aggressively putted his ball six feet past the hole and had to make a difficult uphill putt for his par. Casper narrowly missed his birdie putt and the two men tied for the championship after 72 holes and were bound for an 18-hole playoff the next day.

There is an ingratiating photograph of Casper, with his right arm around Palmer's shoulder, consoling him as the two men walked off the eighteenth green. His compassion for Palmer's collapse didn't dampen Casper's competitive fire. He beat Palmer the next day in the playoff posting a score of 69 to Palmer's 72.

The human mind strains for explanations of catastrophes. There is much rumination about the cause of Palmer's quick fall from grace that Sunday at the U.S. Open. Some commentators said the reason he lost the championship was that he was just too nice a guy. Legend has it that as Palmer and Casper walked down the 10th fairway with Palmer holding what both he and Casper thought was an insurmountable lead, Casper said to his playing partner, "Arnie, I want to finish second." Palmer responded, " I will do everything I can to help you." In retrospect, there is bitterness to the irony of that exchange unparalleled in the annals of sport.

Other prognosticators claim that on those final nine holes, Palmer assumed he had the tournament in hand and continued playing with unnecessary aggression in pursuit of Ben Hogan's all time U.S. Open record score of 276, which Hogan established when he won in 1948 at Riviera Country Club in Los Angeles. Still others claim that he played recklessly because he was convinced that his formidable young rival, Jack Nicklaus would mount a last minute charge and steal the tournament from him (the way he had in 1962 at Oakmont Country Club in Pennsylvania). Nicklaus, in fact, did make a charge, but came up three strokes short and finished third. It was Palmer who finished second.

All these explanations involve one fatal mistake: losing focus of the immediate task at hand. On any summer Saturday afternoon, the media is interviewing players with the lead in a golf tournament and they are all saying the same thing. " Well, tomorrow I'm just going to go out there and play one shot at a time. I'm not going to get ahead of myself. I know there is still a lot of golf to be played and I don't want to lose focus." Perhaps Palmer's most lasting golf lesson is the one he taught by example at the 1966 U. S. Open.

As always, the 18th hole at Olympic played prominently again at the 1987 U.S. Open. In particular, a tall cypress tree, which stood 20 feet from the right edge of the fairway and had grown so that it effectively guarded the right side of the 18th green, achieved particular prominence. In 1987 the presence of the tree added measurably to the difficulty of the final hole. Players had to place their shots on the left side of the fairway in order to have an absolutely clear second shot to the green. This meant that players had to hit a particular shot, a slight draw off the tee. If a player hit the ball too far left he risked finding himself in the left rough with a terrible lie like the ones experienced in the past by Hogan and Palmer. On the other hand, if a player found his ball on the right side of the fairway, he would be forced to negotiate the tree on his second shot. Over the years, as the tree had grown in height, it had become increasingly difficult for players to hit their shots high enough to carry the tree.

Tommy Nakajima, the best professional golfer in Japan at the time, came to the final hole in his third round on Saturday in serious contention for the 1987 U. S. Open championship. He hit his tee shot to the right side of the fairway and then his second shot caught the top limbs of the cypress and the ball remained lodged within the branches of the tree. A couple of young patrons tried to assist him in locating his ball by scaling the tree and although they located a number of golf balls that day, they failed to find his ball and he suffered a two stroke penalty which seriously diminished his chances of winning the championship. A few years later a storm with violent winds felled the cypress. With the absence of the tree, players now have a clear shot at the green from the right side of the fairway.

When the final round of the '87 U. S. Open commenced on Sunday, there were nine players bunched together at the top of the leader board, and all of them had a chance to win the coveted title. After play on the front nine, however, the tournament seemed to be a contest between two players: Tom Watson and Scott Simpson. Watson had bolted his way into contention on Friday by firing a score of 65. He followed up with an even-par round of 71 on Saturday.

As he continued his stellar play on the front nine on Sunday and other players faded under the pressure and severe conditions of the course, Watson seemed poised to perform an exorcism of the evil spirits which haunted the fairways and greens of Olympic and prevented premier contestants from winning U.S. Opens on its unhallowed grounds.

Besides, Watson was receiving good vibes from the gallery. Despite the fact that he lived in Kansas City, Missouri, he was deemed a local favorite because he was a graduate of Stanford University with a degree in psychology. While he was at Stanford he had played the Olympic Club's Lake Course a number of times as a member of Stanford's golf team so he possessed a large degree of "local knowledge" which gave him a significant advantage over other players.

Watson's 38th birthday was in 1987. He was approaching the twilight of a great career. In the early 1980's, Watson had succeeded Jack Nicklaus as golf's premier player in much the same way that Nicklaus had supplanted Palmer in the early 1970's.

In 1987, however, Watson's preeminence was being seriously challenged. His last meaningful victory had been the 1982 U.S. Open at Pebble Beach where his miraculous chip shot on Pebble's 17th hole had snatched a U.S. Open championship from the great Nicklaus. This shot at Pebble has been immortalized by television. Before every U.S. Open the footage of Watson dancing around and around the 17th green at Pebble Beach after the shot is aired incessantly. Since the exuberance of that victory at Pebble, Watson had suffered a number of heartbreaking defeats. The most bitter one coming at the hands of Seve Ballesteros at the 1984 British Open after which Seve imitated one of his native bullfighters in claiming that his victory had "finished Watson." Consequently, it must have delighted Watson that Ballesteros was one of the players who faded early on that Sunday at Olympic. Seve bogeyed three out of his first six holes in that final round and played himself out of contention.

During the 1987 Open, Watson seemed to have regained his old form. After firing a score of 65 in the second round, he told reporters that something had clicked. "It was as if a light switch had been turned on," he commented. Indeed, his swing seemed as smoothly rhythmic as it had been when amassing all those victories in the late 1970's. His putting stroke, however, remained suspect. In his final round that Sunday in 1987, Watson's putting stroke did not let him down. He holed great par-saving putts on both No. 14 and No. 17, and carded a one-under-par score of 70 which was a very respectable score since the average round posted by the rest of the field that day was 75.

In truth, Tom Watson didn't lose the '87 U. S. Open, Scott Simpson, a 31-year-old golf professional from Southern California won the championship. Simpson had attended the University of Southern California on a golf scholarship and was twice the NCCA champion. When he joined the PGA Tour after college great things were expected of him. He was known as a very smart and steady player. His driving distance off the tee was better than average, and his solid iron play positioned him as a top player in terms of hitting greens in regulation. Overall he was an average putter, although his methodical putting style allowed him to sink a high percentage of short putts.

Simpson had played in 13 U.S. Open championships prior to 1987 at Olympic, and he had contended through the third round in a couple of them. Once he found himself in or near the lead, however, his play would immediately deteriorate and he would slip back into the middle of the pack. Although he had won three times on tour, he had never been able to "seal the deal" at a major championship. Everyone assumed history would repeat itself for Simpson in his final round at the Lake Course, yet he was determined to prove them wrong.

He did. Simpson birdied three of the last six holes. His stellar performance on Sunday rivaled the more celebrated U.S. Open final round charges of Jack Nicklaus at the Baltusrol Country Club in 1967 and Johnny Miller at Oakmont in 1973. As Simpson approached the 18th tee that Sunday, he summoned history when he said to himself, "If Jack Fleck could do it, so can I." Simpson played the 18th hole in textbook fashion. He hit a long iron shot to the left center of the fairway away from the hovering cypress tree, which had caused the demise of Nakijima. From there he hit a nine-iron to the center of the green and from there had a stress free two-putt for par.

When Watson arrived at No. 18, he needed a birdie to tie Simpson and force a playoff. Watson hit a long iron positioning his ball within a few feet of where Simpson's tee shot had landed. Rather than hit a nine-iron, Watson decided to hit a pitching wedge instead. It was a slight miscalculation and his ball came up just short of the putting surface. The crowd settled in the natural amphitheatre around the 18th green and waited in hushed silence for Watson to hit yet another miracle shot just as he had five years earlier at the 17th green at Pebble Beach. Watson stroked his putt from off the green firmly and the ball streaked toward the hole, then it inexplicably lost speed and came up just a few inches short. Simpson was the 1987 U.S. Open champion, and Watson had failed to exorcise the demons, which seemed to stir black magic on the games of the most prominent players when playing the Lake Course in the final round of a U.S. Open.

That same black magic was at work again in 1998 when the Olympic Club's Lake Course was the venue for a United States Open Golf Championship. This time it was aided by a diabolical reconstruction of the 18th green, which became a national embarrassment. With the tall cypress tree on the right side of the 18th fairway gone, it was decided to enhance the difficulty of the 18th hole by greatly increasing the downhill slope of the green. As often happens with such tinkering, it was overdone.

Payne Stewart was one of the most popular players on tour. He was also one of the most recognizable figures within the game because of the way he dressed for play. He wore knickers and argyle socks, a flashback to the dapper golf attire of the 1920's. On Sunday rounds he usually donned the colors of the NFL football team nearest the locale of that week's tournament. He made an exception for final rounds in the U.S. Open when he wore red, white and blue in honor of the national championship.

26

Stewart approached the 18th hole on Friday needing a par to shoot a 65 and take a commanding lead midway through the championship. He hit a good tee shot to the middle of the fairway and then hit a brilliant second shot which landed a mere six feet above the hole. Steward barely touched his ball with his putter and watched it graze the lip of the cup. Then in horror and to the shock of millions of golf fans watching on national television, he watched as his ball kept moving until it rolled off the green. Stewart was able to two-putt from where his ball stopped, but the damage was done. He made bogey. He had lost a stroke because of the condition of the green, and as fate would later attest, that stroke was precious.

The severity of the slope of the green combined with its speed was off the charts. Other players suffered similar fates, many of which were documented on television. There is fair and then there is ridiculously unfair. The eighteenth green on the Lake Course quickly earned the reputation as being the latter. The USGA officials and the Olympic Club grounds crew tried to remedy the situation by not double cutting the 18th green on Saturday or Sunday. In addition, the pin placements on the green for the weekend rounds were designed to mitigate the severity of the green's slope.

In golf history there are windows of time between the eras of dominant players. The late 1990's were one of those times. Watson's star had been waning since 1987, and Tiger Woods (who at the age of 21 had just lapped the field by 12 strokes at the 1998 Masters) was a star on the rise. Players like Stewart, Paul Azinger and Curtis Strange were sharing the spotlight with Greg Norman who seemed invincible in regular tour events, but incredibly vulnerable in major golf championships. When he arrived in San Francisco to play in the 1998 U.S. Open; Stewart had already won a U.S. Open championship. He had defeated none other than Scott Simpson at Hazeltine Golf Club in Minnesota in an eighteen-hole playoff to capture the 1991 championship title.

Riding on the crest of his Masters victory, Woods was a pre-tournament favorite. Woods, however, had great difficulty negotiating the severe U.S. Open conditions presented on the course, and finished the tournament ten-over-par and well out of the running for the championship. Jack Nicklaus, at the age of 50, was also in the house. Nicklaus made a 30-foot uphill putt on the eighteenth hole on Friday's second round to make the cut on the number. Nicklaus' chances of winning another major championship were hampered by a worn out hip (which he would soon after have replaced) and he hobbled around the final 36 holes heroically but without the spark necessary to produce a victory.

Another U.S. Open champion, Lee Janzen, was also playing well in the 1998 championship. Janzen had won his U.S. Open title in 1993 at Baltusrol Golf and Country Club in New Jersey. Janzen had won the tournament by two strokes over the colorful Payne Stewart. The two players and their respective families had become friends and often enjoyed each other's company as they traveled from tournament to tournament on the PGA Tour.

Janzen started his final round five strokes behind Stewart who led the tournament. He got off to a fast start with birdies on two of the first four holes. Then, on the fifth hole his drive (the high fade called for by the shape of the hole) drifted into the grove of trees bordering the right-hand fairway. His ball caught a branch and stayed lodged there. Just as Janzen was about to return to the tee to hit another drive and suffer a two-stroke penalty, a gust of wind whistled through the trees and his ball dropped down into the fairway. Janzen proceeded to par the hole and maintain the momentum of his final round. He birdied three of the next 13 holes and suffered no bogeys and posted a final score of 68.

Stewart, on the other hand, suffered a number of unlucky breaks, which caused him to lose ground to par. For example, on the par-4 twelfth hole, he hit a beautiful drive into the center of the fairway only to find it lodged in a divot hole, which resulted in a bogey on the hole. As he labored toward the finish, three of his putts tickled the lip of the hole but refused to drop in. Despite the beguiling black magic, which seemed to engulf his play, Stewart had a 20-foot birdie putt on the 18th hole to tie Janzen and force an 18-hole playoff the next day. As had been the order of the day, his putt narrowly missed and Janzen was again a U.S. Open champion.

There was no joy at the presentation ceremony, which immediately followed on the 18th green. Both Janzen, the winner, and Stewart, the runner up, were present, joined by their wives. Everyone was crying. A teary-eyed Janzen sheepishly raised the trophy level with his head as he told reporters that the 1998 U.S. Open champion should have been Payne Stewart. Janzen and his wife were consoling Payne and his wife for coming up a shot short, and Stewart and his wife were consoling Janzen and his wife for Lee having won a championship, which Janzen felt belonged to his friend, Payne.

Payne Stewart would proceed to win a second U.S. Open at Pinehurst Golf Club & Resort the following year. He would come to the 18th hole at that course needing a par to win the tournament. He mis-hit his tee shot into the heavy, right-hand rough and would have to play out of the rough into the middle of the fairway to a point one hundred and twenty yards from the green. From there he solidly hit a nine-iron shot twenty feet below the pin. He had a slightly uphill putt for the win. As he stood over that putt he must have summoned memories of the twenty-foot putt he had at the Olympic Club a year earlier. His calm, yet determined demeanor, over his putt at Pinehurst signaled his faith that this was his time and fate would finally turn in his favor, and it did. The putt rolled solidly into the middle of the cup and Payne expressed an elation, which is chronicled as one of the monumental moments in U.S. Open history.

There is another, more touching scene, which immediately followed Payne's initial euphoria. It is Payne, face to face, with Phil Mickelson, consoling him as the runner up, but more importantly telling him that he should be elated because Phil was about to become a father for the first time. Through this gesture, Payne was telling Phil that championships are great, but the real joys in life, the ones that last, are family and fatherhood.

Sadly, four months after his triumph at Pinehurst, Payne would die in a tragic airplane accident over the hills of South Dakota. His friend and fellow competitor, Lee Janzen, now mentors Payne's son in his efforts to excel at the game his fatherloved so very much and played which such grace and courage.

Despite its reputation for being an unkind venue to golf's greatest players, the U.S. Open is scheduled to be played again at the Olympic Club in 2012. The course has been tweaked to accommodate the championship. For example, the infamous slope of the 18th green has been considerably reduced so that downhill putts are not so ridiculously slick as to prompt national ridicule. The eighth hole has been changed so that it is longer and more challenging. A few other holes have been lengthened to accommodate the improved technology of both golf clubs and golf balls. The fundamental layout of the course, however, remains the same and as challenging as it was for its previous four U.S. Open Championships.

As the tournament nears, golf enthusiasts love to speculate as to what might happen at Olympic's infamous venue in 2012. Will Tiger Woods find redemption by exorcising both his personal demons and the black magic, which seems to thwart great players at U.S. Opens played at the Olympic Club? Will Phil Mickelson put to rest his haunting memories of U.S. Open defeats at Wing Foot and Pinehurst and finally win the championship in which he has finished as the runner up a record six times?

Or will the Olympic Club prove true to its history and produce another unsung champion, who on that particular week mysteriously elevates his play to claim the U.S. Open champion title? As these questions persist, the 18th hole at Olympic beckons.

Quick Order Form

To order additional copies of
"The 18th Hole", please go:

online   visit www.thewrongguyalwayswinsatolymic.com
                       (includes amazon, kindle, iPad, etc.)
by email   orders@thewrongguyalwayswinsatolymic.com
by phone   650.960.3772
by fax   650.960.3773 (use this form)
by mail   be here now books, P.O. Box 3776, Los Altos, CA 94024

Questions?   visit www.thewrongguyalwayswinsatolymic.com

The 18th Hole
$9.95 US/ $13.95 CAN   ISBN 978-0-9833882-1-0

_____# Books x $9.95 = $_____   + shipping= $_____
Order Total = $_____

Sales tax: Please add 9.25% for products shipped to California addresses
Shipping: USA- $5.00 for the first book; add $2.50 for each additional item
International: $12.00 for the first book: $5.00 for each additional item (estimate)

Printable e-Book (immediate download) available at
www.thewrongguyalwayswinsatolymic.com

Billing/Shipping Information:
Full Name: _____
Address: _____
City: _____ State: _____Zip: _____
Phone: _____
Email: _____

Payment Information:
Name on Card: _____
Card Type:_____
Card#: _____
Exp. Date: _____ / _____ (MM/YYYY) CV2# _____

www.ingramcontent.com/pod-product-compliance
Lightning Source LLC
Chambersburg PA
CBHW061654050426
42443CB00027B/3294